Leadership L

LEADERSHIP
LESSONS
from
Dad

Father always knows best!

Peter R. Garber

HRD Press, Inc. • Amherst • Massachusetts

Copyright © 2006, Peter Garber

Published by:

HRD Press
22 Amherst Road
Amherst, MA 01002
1-800-822-2801
(U.S. and Canada)
1-413-253-3488
1-413-253-3490 (Fax)
www.hrdpress.com

ISBN 0-87425-876-6

Cover design by Eileen Klockars
Productions services by PerfectType
Editorial services by Suzanne Bay

About the
Leadership Lessons from Life Series

The most important and significant things we learn about life are usually basic and fundamental lessons taught to us early on—lessons that we might have forgotten about, overlooked, or simply taken for granted. Even the most complicated leadership theory has as its source something we were taught when we were young. The ***Leadership Lessons from Life*** series is designed to remind us of this wisdom and help us apply it to our efforts to become better, more-effective leaders.

Each book in the series is devoted to exploring what we learn from significant people or events in our lives as it relates to our professional endeavors. Even the most challenging leadership and management situations can be changed for the better as a result of insights coming from unexpected sources. As you read each book, you will have a new appreciation for this simple wisdom and find new ways to apply the fundamental principles to your professional life and responsibilities.

Good luck in your never-ending learning journey. May this ***Leadership Lessons from Life*** series make the experience valuable and enjoyable.

Introduction

All fathers have one main goal when it comes to raising children: to prepare their sons and daughters to go out into the world and take care of themselves. Fathers use their life experience and wisdom to help their kids grow and learn, and they put most of their efforts into turning them into strong, self-reliant individuals who can make their own way in life.

Most of us remember times during childhood when we struggled with a problem while Dad just sat there and watched us grapple with it. Whether it was the science project that was put off until the night before it was due or the dents we put in the neighbor's car, we were left to solve the problem on our own. If you're a parent now (and even if you're not), you know how hard it was for your father not to intervene and get you out of your jam. He no doubt predicted the outcome, yet he said nothing, letting you learn your lesson the hard way—by suffering the consequences all by yourself. Dads seem to have an innate sense of when to step in and give their children advice or help, and when to hold back and let them learn life's lessons for themselves.

What we learn from fathers is passed down from generation to generation. The lessons themselves are taught in a variety of different ways according to our age and circumstance. Some take us years to truly learn, but many more we apply throughout our lives, without realizing where they came from. This book is a reminder of the special wisdom passed on to us by fathers and grandfathers everywhere that can help us succeed in our professional lives. They are worth remembering, even now.

Leadership Lesson #1

Be honest.

Honesty is one of the most important character traits fathers try to help their children develop. The father of our country, George Washington, was taught by his father to speak the truth in everything. As children, we were told that young George had to confess to his dad that he was the one who chopped down that infamous cherry tree, knowing he would suffer punishment for the act. Whether or not there is any truth to the story, it is still told to generations of schoolchildren so they will learn to tell the truth, even when they know they will get into trouble. Fathers seem to feel especially responsible for teaching their children the importance of honesty. Even a little "white" lie was considered wrong. There was no such thing as compromise when it came to telling the truth.

When we reach our teens, we really begin to understand just how important honesty is in our lives. Seeing other kids cheat on exams, shoplift, or use illegal drugs just to have fun all cause us to examine issues of right and wrong. Eventually we learn that honesty is a fundamental principle in building character and morality. In an ideal world, everyone is honest and there are no ethical or business scandals making the headlines. Wouldn't life be so much less complicated if everyone just followed their father's advice about being honest?

Well, it isn't an ideal world, and your organization is counting on you to make Dad's lessons about honesty part of "the way things are done around here." A leader must be a positive role model for honesty. Your dad exemplified what he preached, didn't he? Employees look to their leaders to explain (and follow) the rules of the organization, but also need to know how the rules are bent or interpreted. They learn from you whether or not telling just a little fib is acceptable. This is perhaps where the true standards for honesty in an organization are established and reinforced: In the leader. You set the example for others. Don't expect those you lead to be more honest than you are. Be consistently honest in all your business dealings, and expect everyone you supervise to act in the same manner.

Leadership Tips

- Set the example for honesty in the workplace.

- Make sure that everyone understands why honesty is so important to the organization.

- Don't condone or reinforce actions or behaviors that are dishonest or unethical.

- Make sure that honesty and trustworthiness are key operating principles in your organization. This might require you to make difficult decisions that truly support your commitment to honesty.

- Publicly and privately, reward employee honesty.

Even a little white lie was wrong, according to Dad—for him, there was no such thing as compromise when it came to telling the truth.

Leadership Lesson #2

Have integrity.

Integrity is a little harder to teach than most lessons we learned from our fathers. We use the term to refer to a firm adherence to a code of moral values. Integrity is about honesty, truthfulness, incorruptibility, honor, and reliability—basically, *you know it when you see it.* Fathers want to instill a sense of integrity in their children; it is a basic building block of character, respect, and success in life. One of the most important goals for any father is to teach his children how to develop integrity.

This incorruptibility is sorely needed in the world of work and business, as well as in life. The success of any organization is based in large measure on what it values and how honest it is as it pursues its goals. A reputation for integrity is one of the most valuable assets an organization has. Integrity cannot be bought or inherited or acquired overnight; it takes great effort and time to earn a reputation as an honorable and reliable organization. And it can be damaged or even destroyed by just one unethical or dishonest act.

Well-respected leaders possess integrity and demonstrate it in everything they say and do. Leaders are really the *watchdogs* of the organization's integrity, so they must insist that it be the basis of every business decision and action they are responsible for. Integrity must begin at the top and become a guiding principle for the rest of the organization. Dads show us how it's done; now it's our turn.

Leadership Tips

- ◉ The organization itself has to clearly state the importance of integrity at every level, and exemplify it consistently.

- ◉ Develop a written policy that clearly states the organization's position on issues concerning integrity and ethical business conduct, and make sure each employee understands that policy.

- ◉ Remember that an organization's true worth is ultimately measured by its reputation for integrity.

- ◉ Insist that every employee act with integrity each and every day. There are no exceptions or free passes when it comes to integrity; you must never take a day off from working at it.

It takes great effort
and time to earn a
reputation for integrity,
but one unethical or
dishonest act can
damage and even
destroy it.

Leadership Lesson #3

Build trust.

"Trust" is a very important word in every father's vocabulary, particularly when it comes to children. Parents know that they cannot spend every waking moment protecting and guiding their children, so they stress trust as a way to remind them to obey their rules when they are not present. A father also wants his children to learn to trust others, such as friends and teachers. Trust in ourselves and in others is a basic principle in life that helps us move ahead, even in times of uncertainty and doubt.

Every employee needs to be able to trust his or her employer and supervisors, but this is a more complicated trusting relationship than the one that takes place in families. This kind of trust is conditional, based on the current and longer-term needs of both the employee and the organization. The conditions of this trust can change, depending on the state of the business or even the direction of the organization. Organizations are merging, downsizing, globalizing, and reorganizing with unpredictable frequency. Trust is all too rare in many of today's organizations.

As a leader, you need to help employees develop trust in the organization by first earning and deserving their trust, and then by showing them where and with whom they should place their trust. In fact, creating a climate of trust throughout the organization might be the most important thing you do as a leader. Organizations built on trust operate much more effectively and efficiently because their employees believe it has been earned.

Leadership Tips

- ▶ Stress that trust is an important element in any relationship, and most importantly, a professional one.

- ▶ Find ways to build trust among employees at all levels.

- ▶ Help employees understand where to place their trust within the organization.

- ▶ Demonstrate consistently that you believe an organization without trust makes for a very insecure workforce and uncomfortable workplace, and that your organization will work hard to deserve that trust.

- ▶ Remember that trust works both ways: You have to trust others if you want to earn their trust.

Create a climate
of trust throughout
the organization.
It might be the most
important thing you
do as a leader.

Leadership Lesson #4

Work hard.

Dads teach their children that if they want to get anywhere in life, they have to be prepared to work hard. Hard work, they stress, is the only road to success. Fathers tend to frown on life strategies that are based on anything else but working hard and doing your best. "Don't expect anyone to hand you success. You have to *earn* it!" our dads tell us, starting when we are very young. They take every opportunity to get us to adopt this work ethic, no matter how old we are.

Dad was right. You can't expect to be handed success; you have to earn it each and every day you go to work. The lesson is as timeless as the ages, isn't it? When our spirits flag and we lose confidence in ourselves, fathers step in and remind us that we must be patient. Hard work doesn't always pay off (at least not right away), and success doesn't happen overnight. It takes time.

As a leader, you have undoubtedly had to remind employees of the virtues of hard work and the need to be patient to reap its rewards. It can be frustrating when we don't get the results we expected. Be sure you reassure your employees that their efforts are not wasted—that staying focused on the task will eventually result in a positive outcome. Dad showed you how to give that same kind of encouragement.

Leadership Tips

- Make sure that employees know that you recognize all their hard work and effort to get the job done. Convey your appreciation frequently.

- Keep reassuring individual employees that their efforts will result in a positive outcome.

- Acknowledge interim steps or accomplishments that employees achieve along the way to the goal.

- Give special recognition to each employee when he or she has finally achieved a goal that has required diligence and particular effort.

Success doesn't happen overnight. Make sure you acknowledge interim accomplishments.

Leadership Lesson #5

Stand up for yourself.

This next lesson confused us when we were kids. Do you remember being told by your parents to do what you were told? Then you came home from school upset because a bully was picking on little kids, and you thought you would be next. Your dad told you to stand up for yourself, but how do you do that in every situation and at the same time be polite and respectful? It's not that these concepts are mutually exclusive; it's just that the lines between them were blurred. The secret, Dad explained, is to stand up for yourself when you need to do so in a respectful and appropriate manner. Your father might have said something like, "Approach has everything to do with success." His lesson was that it is *how* you say or do something that is ultimately more important than *what* you say or do. Stand your ground, but don't do it in a way that detracts from the message that you want to get across. That is, unless you need to stand up for yourself when the schoolyard bully comes around!

Everyone at every level needs to be given opportunities to express themselves and share their opinions. This can only happen in a work culture and environment that allows people to feel comfortable respectfully saying what's on their minds and expressing what's important to them as individuals. They need to be able to stand up for themselves and tell managers and supervisors how they feel about issues involving the organization and their role in it. This will ultimately create a more healthy and productive workplace.

If you don't work in this kind of environment, then you need to create one. Your responsibility is to make people feel that they can share their ideas and opinions without risk to their careers. However, there do need to be some parameters or acceptable standards. Establish formal and informal ways that employees can express how they feel about their jobs and the workplace in order to improve the organization.

Leadership Tips

- Consider establishing a "hotline" or e-mail mailbox for employees who want to talk (even anonymously) about organizational problems or concerns.

- Set aside time for employees to discuss their career or work concerns with decisionmakers.

- Make sure that employees have regular opportunities to discuss career and job issues of particular interest to the individual, particularly during performance appraisals.

- Don't shoot the messenger. Employees who stand up for themselves in an acceptable and appropriate manner and express concern about workplace issues should not suffer any recriminations for doing so.

- Remember that just listening to these issues is very important, particularly to the individual expressing concern. Try to understand what is truly important to individual employees.

Stand your ground,
but don't do it in such
a way that it detracts
from the message that
you want to get across.

Leadership Lesson #6

Obey the rules.

Rules are very important to fathers; they believe that it is their responsibility to make sure their children learn to obey the family rules before they grow up.

Of course, respecting and obeying the rules as adults is also very important. Every organization has rules that must be followed. Some rules are informal and relatively benign, while others are seriously significant. The informal rules of an organization are often not written down—they tend to be a part of the culture of the organization or corporation, handed down by word of mouth (often after you break them).

Helping employees understand the rules and how they are to be followed is a leadership responsibility, as is enforcing them fairly and equitably. Employees who do their best to respect the rules of the organization become angry and discouraged if they see that others are being allowed to break the rules without consequence. Remember what your dad taught you about integrity and trust as you enforce the rules of the organization consistently and fairly.

Leadership Tips

- Make sure that all the formal rules of the organization are written down and distributed to each employee.

- Keep employees in your organization up-to-date on any rule changes.

- Make yourself available to discuss how to interpret these rules.

- Speak to employees frequently about the formal rules of the organization (as well as the informal rules) and the reasons for them. Prevent any misunderstanding by providing feedback on how they're doing.

The rules get bigger and more important as we grow, and so do the consequences.

Leadership Lesson #7

Experience is the best teacher.

Experience is everything to fathers. They use their own life experiences to teach their children about the world as they grow. Dads relate their personal experiences and lessons they have learned to whatever it is that their children are experiencing at the time—a stunning defeat on the ballfield, the invitation to a big party that never arrived, a failing grade on a pop quiz. Sometimes kids don't want to hear another one of Dad's *stories,* but as they grow older, they become more interested and even start to appreciate the importance of those lessons. Experience really is the best teacher—especially when it is Dad's experience, shared at just the right moment.

In the work world, experience is also our best teacher. Listen to the voice of experience; some skills can only be learned and mastered after several trials and many errors. Be sure your employees at all levels see you learning from your mistakes, so they will learn to respect the experience of those who have been doing the job for a long time.

There are probably individuals in your organization who have more experience than you—not necessarily the exact same experiences, but wisdom and perspective that has been acquired over the years. Listen carefully to these experienced people: They can give you great advice based on what they have gone through in their own lives, saving you the cost of mistakes as you learn these lessons. Avoid the arrogance of power and position: Not only is it isolating, but it prevents others from teaching you things you didn't know you didn't know. You can learn a great deal from those who report to you. When they tell you about the lessons they have learned from their own lives, listen carefully. One of them might give you the best leadership advice you will ever receive!

Leadership Tips

- Seek the advice of those more experienced than you.

- Find people with experience throughout the organization—even direct reports and retirees. Ask for their advice and perspective, and listen closely.

- When you're trying to solve a problem, think about who might have been through a similar situation in the past. Seek out their advice.

- Write down the advice you receive from others more experienced than you, so you can refer back to it in the future.

- Share this advice with others.

You can learn a great
deal from the people
you manage or
supervise.
Listen to them.

Leadership Lesson # 8

Make your own way in the world.

Every dad teaches his children not to expect to be handed anything on a silver platter. *You have to make your own way in the world.* Dads are famous for saying things like, "You can't expect to have success handed to you," or "If you wait for someone to cut you a break, you'll be waiting a long time. You've got to make your own breaks in life." And, of course, Dad was right. However, in reality, the key advantages we do get in life come from our fathers: the advice, support, guidance, and everything else we needed to grow into the adults we are today.

Employees in today's competitive world shouldn't expect to be given any break when it comes to work. They need to compete and *earn* the rewards and advantages. But they must also know what it will take to achieve these goals. It is not fair to expect an individual to put the effort into trying to meet a challenge unless you tell him or her how it can be done and provide regular feedback on their progress.

The leader needs to make sure that each person understands what he or she has to do personally to be successful in your organization. Have feedback systems in place so that employees at all levels of the organization understand how well they are performing their jobs and understand which areas they need to improve. Then make sure they can access the resources needed to improve. Remember, however, that feedback and coaching have to be provided on an ongoing, daily basis—not just once a year during a formal performance evaluation.

Leadership Tips

- Make sure that each individual employee understands the requirements of his or her job.

- Explain the performance standards each employee is expected to meet at work, as well as the criteria for advancement.

- Make sure each employee receives formal feedback on their performance on a regular basis. Their supervisor should provide this feedback.

- See to it that employees receive informal feedback in the form of day-to-day coaching, and be sure the organization provides opportunities to acquire new skills.

Make sure that everyone understands what they have to do in order to be successful in your organization.

Leadership Lesson # 9

Take care of your family.

Fathers have a strong sense of responsibility when it comes to their families. They want to take care of everyone and provide for as many of their children's needs as possible, and pretty much dedicate their lives to achieving this objective. This innate sense of responsibility is usually passed on to their children so that they can succeed in their chosen careers, but also so they remember and understand the importance of family.

It is often said that to be truly happy and successful in life, we have to achieve a good balance between career and family. Becoming a CEO of a Fortune 500 company or the firm's top sales director at the expense of your family is not what most people consider "success." Becoming too focused on your career goals can, in fact, be the cause of many personal problems. It can even affect your health and well-being.

Leaders need to think more like fathers, and make allowances for their employees' needs when it comes to family.

There will be times when a worker's responsibility to his or her family needs to take precedence: a serious illness, a championship spelling bee, or a spouse's business trip might impose unusual demands on employees. Leaders must be aware of and sensitive to these critically important moments in their employees' lives, and be supportive of the individual's desire to balance their work and family responsibilities.

Leadership Tips

- Try to get your organization to sponsor activities and programs for employees and their families that will help them maintain a healthy work/life balance.

- Encourage employees and their families to participate in these kinds of activities.

- Remember that your participation will also encourage employees to participate.

- Be sure you are completely knowledgeable about the policies your organization has in place to help employees and their families during difficult times in their lives. Make sure these benefits are made available to workers in a timely manner.

Remember that there will be times when an employee's responsibility to his or her family needs to take precedence over their job.

Leadership Lesson # 10

Be determined.

Dads are often great role models for determination. Their success in life was likely achieved as a result of their determination, and they try to use these life experiences to teach their children not to give up pursuing a goal—even a modest one. Determination, every father will tell you, can overcome many of life's obstacles.

Leaders also understand how important a sense of determination is in achieving success in organizations. Most goals worth achieving are difficult to reach, which is what makes them so valuable and desired. But just having the ability and the desire is usually not enough—you also have to be determined to stick with it, and to do whatever it takes to get the job done.

Leaders need to get this across to their employees. *How much commitment must be made in order to reach this goal?* If workers have a realistic understanding of what it will take, they can decide for themselves whether or not they want to make that commitment. The requirements and efforts necessary to achieve success must be the same for every employee, however; do not hold people to different standards, or you will alienate and discourage them from taking on other challenges.

Leadership Tips

- Define what is required for every goal and opportunity in the organization, and communicate these details to all employees.

- If an employee decides to pursue a longer-term goal, be sure to support them in every way possible.

- Make sure that the standards and requirements for goal achievement are the same for all employees.

- Recognize and accept an employee's personal decision not to go after a career goal.

- Find ways to celebrate goal achievements with the whole team.

Determination, every father will tell you, can overcome many of life's obstacles.

Leadership Lesson # 11

Don't skip the School of Hard Knocks.

Fathers often speak of the *School of Hard Knocks*. No one really knows where this school of hard knocks is—just that his or her father was a student there at one time. But there are very important and valuable lessons taught in this institution; in fact, it is where dads learn many of the most important lessons in life. The curriculum consists of difficult experiences and challenges, as well as mistakes. Every father wants his children to learn from his mistakes, as well as their own.

Despite your father's desire to spare you from the same problems he had in his life, you have already faced your share of challenges along the way. You probably took a class or two at the same school of hard knocks your father attended. That's what your father really wanted for you: to learn how to effectively deal with and manage life's challenges by negotiating through a few bumps and ruts in the road. This is a very important and necessary lesson to learn. It also builds character.

Leaders can't possibly protect their employees from everything, but what they can do is help employees learn to effectively deal with the challenges that they must face. Provide encouragement, advice, and perhaps even resources to deal with these problems, but try to remember that it is ultimately each employee's responsibility to learn to resolve work-related problems and challenges on their own. The goal is to learn from our mistakes and personal trials, and to grow and develop from each experience.

Leadership Tips

- Help people tackle challenges and solve problems, but don't make them dependent on you to fix everything.

- Do what you can to help an employee, but make sure the individual understands that it is his responsibility to solve *his* problem.

- Help employees learn from difficult or challenging work experiences.

- Talk informally with employees about what they are learning from their most difficult experiences and how they think these lessons will help them in the future.

No one really
knows where this
School of Hard Knocks
is located—just that
Dad was a
student there.

Leadership Lesson #12

Learn how to do things right.

Your father wanted you to learn how to do things right. He probably said something like, "It is easier to do something right the first time than to do it over later on. Write an essay, mow the lawn, run the dishwasher, clean the fish tank— whatever the situation or activity, the real lesson he was teaching you was to set performance standards for yourself, and try to meet them every time.

There are also standards at work that must be followed precisely. Doing the job right is important in any position, and many times there is little or no margin for error. Employers have every right to expect a job to be performed correctly; after all, that is what they are paying you for. Mistakes cost organizations money and customers.

Leaders need to insist on quality performance throughout the organization. Start by making sure that employees know how to perform their jobs correctly. Establish processes for each task and train each worker in proper procedures. Make sure that they fully understand the cost of making mistakes.

Leadership Tips

- Make sure that the requirements and performance standards for each job are understood by those performing the duties.

- Train each employee in the correct processes and make sure they have what they need to do their job right.

- Try to find out why something isn't being done right—as soon as possible.

- Find out if the organization's operating systems are capable of achieving this objective, or whether or not changes will need to be made to correct the problem.

Make sure that each employee knows how to perform his or her job correctly. Establish procedures and periodic checks.

Leadership Lesson #13

Do the right things.

It is important to do things right, but it is also important to do the right things. No matter how well or how effectively you do something, if you aren't doing the *right* thing, you aren't really accomplishing anything. Dads are particularly skilled at spotting the difference between these two concepts. They don't want to see their children work hard at something only to become frustrated and discouraged because they were working on the wrong things. Learning how to make good decisions about where we put our efforts during our lifetime is an important lesson. However, convincing anyone that they are going down the wrong path in life is a challenge— even for dads.

Getting people in an organization to do the right things can be equally challenging. There are many paths that can be followed, but only a few will lead to success. Unfortunately, it is not always apparent which path will lead you to do the *right* things.

It is up to the leader to help employees understand what the *right* thing is, and then provide guidance and direction concerning the path forward. It should coincide with the vision a leader has for the organization. Communicating this vision so that everyone has a better understanding of where the organization is headed will help employees determine which paths to take.

Leadership Tips

- Be sure that everyone in the organization understands the difference between doing things right and doing the right things.

- Create a plan that spells out what people are expected to do, and explain and reinforce it regularly so people maintain their focus.

- While you are emphasizing the importance of doing the right things, go over the correct ways of doing them (doing things right).

It is not only
important to do
things right, but also
to do the right things.

Leadership Lesson #14

Show respect.

Fathers teach their children to respect other people, and they expect their children to treat them with respect as well. Showing respect is a great compliment: We are demonstrating that we see important attributes in that individual and hold him or her in high regard. Fathers understand the true value of the word. They have worked their entire lives to try to earn the respect of others, and along the way, they learned that it is not achieved, but *earned.* They want their children to respect people who deserve their esteem and to demonstrate that respect.

Respect is something that there is too little of in the workplace. Many interpersonal conflicts would be prevented if all employees treated one another with consideration. It starts with the individual, however: The way we treat others is often the way they in turn will treat us. You get what you give when it comes to respect.

Respect is especially important with a diverse workforce composed of people from other cultures, ethnicities, or religious groups who struggle to adapt to unfamiliar rules and traditions. There are many advantages to having a multicultural workforce, as long as leaders set the right tone by encouraging and demonstrating understanding, respect, and support.

ost organizations already have policies that are based on
pect for the organization and its employees. When these
rules are not followed, the leader must take action. It is the
leader's responsibility to create a culture of workplace respect
and consideration; if you do not have formal policies that
establish such a culture, make it a priority to develop them.

Leadership Tips

- Develop policies and practices in your organization
  that address issues arising from lack of respect. Make
  sure they are understood and adhered to.

- Sponsor or create diversity programs that encourage
  understanding and acceptance of the differences that
  exist among employees, and communicate the ways
  that this diversity enriches the organization.

- Provide support systems to help individuals who are
  having problems getting along with others to find
  more positive ways to deal with interpersonal conflict.

Organizations greatly benefit from having diversity programs that encourage understanding and respect for the differences in people.

Leadership Lesson # 15

Stick to your convictions.

Dads teach their children to stand up for what they believe in. They tell us that if we are totally committed to something, we shouldn't let anyone or anything discourage us. Some things require us to *stand our ground,* despite pressures to change our position—they're that important.

Our commitments and our values are often challenged as we go through life. Sometimes we must make a decision that goes against our convictions or sense of right and wrong; these are the times when we need to remember our dad's sage advice about standing up for what we believe in.

As a leader, you need to stick to your convictions as well. *Stand your ground* when it comes to the values and principles that you and your organization stand for. Compromising your principles in order to solve a current problem is likely to lead to more problems later on down the road.

Leadership Tips

- Make sure that the organization's values and principles are clearly established and communicated to all employees.

- Use these values and principles to guide you as you make important leadership decisions.

- Don't compromise these principles and values, even if you have to make difficult decisions as a result.

- Remember that you are a role model for others in your organization when it comes to values and principles. Put your money where your mouth is.

Stand your ground
when it comes to the
values and principles
you and your
organization stand for.

Leadership Lesson # 16

Take responsibility.

Fathers know that they won't always be there to assume responsibility for their children, so they focus all their energies on raising their sons and daughters to have sense of responsibility for themselves. Being able to handle responsibility is one of the most important things that a child needs to learn in order to become a successful adult, but it is a complicated lesson because responsibility involves many things. Honoring our obligations and commitments and being accountable for our actions are two important aspects.

Work is all about responsibility. Each job has specific demands that must be met by the individual, but there are countless occasions when we must depend on other people to accomplish a job task or fulfill broad responsibilities. When one worker fails to meet his or her responsibility at work, the entire system can suffer or even break down.

Leaders have their own responsibilities, one of which is to make sure that employees do what they are assigned to do (sometimes all we need is a little push). Each person's responsibilities must be clearly established and understood, however; leaders should never keep expectations to themselves. It isn't fair or productive to expect an individual to fulfill a responsibility that hasn't been shared or established or understood. That said, be generous with praise and appreciation when you see someone putting in a good effort.

This will give them the confidence they need to take on more responsibility in the future. Just remember how dads do it with their children, and *you'll* probably get it right, too.

Leadership Tips

● Make sure that each person you lead understands his or her job responsibilities.

● Make sure you keep accountability documents, job descriptions, position evaluations, and so on current to reflect these responsibilities.

● Be available and open to discussing individuals' responsibilities and how they feel about their performance.

● Listen to people's ideas about how their job responsibilities can be made more meaningful and productive.

● Be generous with praise and encouragement.

A leader should always let employees know what is expected from them.

Leadership Lesson # 17

Listen to others.

Fathers are always telling their children to listen carefully to what they are being told, but their true message is sometimes hidden beneath the surface. Dads try to teach us about the world through stories and personal experiences, told in their own words. As time goes on, we remember bits and pieces of those talks and wish we had been better listeners (and learners) so we could remember it all.

Listening is a critical job skill. We learn a great deal about people, about the organization, and about the industry by listening, and this can translate into improved performance. Did you know that the best communicators are the best listeners? What keeps the rest of us from becoming good communicators is our tendency to focus more on what *we* have to say, rather than on what *others* have to say. We think about how we want to respond when we are really supposed to be listening to the other person.

A good leader is a good listener who has learned how to lead by listening to the ideas and opinions of others. A leader who doesn't seek input before making important decisions fails to use one of the most valuable resources available—the experience and opinions of colleagues and direct reports. The quality of each decision rises or falls on the quality of the information it is based on, and listening is key. You never know where your next piece of wisdom will come from, so pay attention. That's what Dad was trying to say.

Leadership Tips

- Leaders need to reassure employees that their ideas and opinions are important to the organization. A good way to start the process is to ask, "What do *you* think about this?"

- Set the example. The more you listen, the more you will be listened to!

- Help others in the organization become better listeners; it is a good investment that will pay many dividends.

- You have two ears and one mouth. Remember to use them proportionally.

As we grow older, we regret not listening more closely to the many lessons Dad was trying to teach us.

Leadership Lesson # 18

Keep your word.

"You're only as good as your word." Do you remember your father ever saying that to you or your siblings? Dads want their kids to understand that they should never make promises that they can't keep, and that if a promise is made, they must do everything they can to follow through. Children test this principle early on by saying things like, "Dad, if you let me do this one thing, I promise I will (take out the trash, do the dishes, etc.)." Kids don't always intend to honor their commitments, and dads know this from their own experience. The stage is set for a very important lesson about personal honor.

Of course, keeping your word as an adult is even more important. The consequences are greater, and sometimes there are legal ramifications if you do not deliver on your promises. Your word is the basis for the trust that others have in you, and trust is a necessary ingredient in respect.

We need to believe in and trust our leaders. A leader's words, in fact, are his or her most powerful tools. Be careful about how you use these tools, because the people you lead take them very seriously. A leader cannot truly lead if he or she is not believed or trusted. Once the word gets around that you don't follow through on what you promise to do or that you say one thing to one employee and something different to another, you lose more than the respect and trust of your people—you lose a good reputation. Live up to each and every one of your promises and commitments. Remember what your dad said, and don't let people down.

Leadership Tips

- ▶ Think about just how important your words are to those you lead.

- ▶ Don't say things that you don't mean and don't make promises you might not be able to keep.

- ▶ Honor your word by keeping your commitments.

- ▶ Expect each person in the organization to keep their word, and tell them that.

A leader's words are
his or her most
powerful tools.

Leadership Lesson # 19

Develop resilience.

We all have to have a certain amount of resilience to make it through life. Fathers help their kids understand this as they experience the first of life's many disappointments. They say things like, "You'll do better next time," or "Tomorrow is another day" to help put things in proper perspective. Dads teach us that what looks like a big disappointment today will soon become incidental and forgotten.

Resilience is a quality most adults don't have enough of. Instead of keeping things in perspective and not letting emotions get out of control, many adults start blaming others or acting out in negative ways, thus making the problem bigger than it is. We must learn how to handle setbacks and start to think of disappointments and even failures as challenges or learning opportunities. It is these experiences that build character and make us stronger. They help us become successful and effective leaders.

Leaders are responsible for helping their organizations become collectively resilient. They are the ones who must show employees at all levels how to deal with disappointments and setbacks and encourage them to learn from these experiences. Things won't always go as planned or expected! Keep everyone positive and motivated—even during discouraging times. It will be one of your greatest and rewarding challenges.

Leadership Tips

● Listen to people. Let them express how they feel about disappointments at work.

● Share your perspective on adversity or setbacks that the organization is experiencing, and encourage people to be challenged by the experience.

● Get others involved in developing and executing recovery plans to turn the challenge into an opportunity.

● Learn as much as you can about what caused the disappointment or setback, and use this information to help move the organization forward.

Dads teach us how to think of setbacks and disappointments as learning opportunities.

Leadership Lesson # 20

Develop self-confidence.

Perhaps more than anything else, a father's hope is that his children will go out in the world with confidence in themselves and in others. Fathers hope with all their hearts that they have taught their children everything they need to feel confident that they will be able to handle the challenges that lie ahead.

Personal and professional confidence can make the difference between a mediocre career and an outstanding one. Confidence in our strengths, abilities, determination, and so on lead to success. This conviction that *I can do it* helps us achieve.

Effective leaders are confident that they can successfully lead, but also believe that they can instill self-confidence in others. How? By letting them know they are doing a good job on a task as soon as possible, and by giving them frequent and regular constructive feedback. A leader must also make sure that each individual employee has the training and resources they need to confidently and comfortably perform their jobs to the best of their ability.

Leadership Tips

- Publicly recognize employees who are doing a good job, and pay special attention to work teams.

- Let individuals know how much you respect their abilities and talents.

- Provide opportunities for additional training and professional development so that your employees have the skills to meet present and anticipated organizational needs.

- Show that you are confident in your own leadership ability, but keep building your own skills. Seek out and take advantage of development opportunities for yourself.

Self-confidence
can make the
difference between
having a mediocre
career and having an
outstanding one.

Leadership Lesson # 21

Have faith in others.

Every father wants his children to have a sense of faith and trust, but it is a difficult thing to teach. There are so many things in life that cause us to have doubt. Faith is a deep and strong conviction, belief, or trust, and it only comes from within. Dads teach us that faith is most important during times of doubt and uncertainty, because so often it is the only thing that pulls us through.

Now that we have become adults, we see our faith tested every day. We place our trust in other people and in ourselves, and sometimes we know it's a risky proposition from the get-go. We convince ourselves that the project we have worked so hard on for so long will turn out the way we want, even though the last one went up in smoke. And there are even times when we doubt our own ability to get a job done on time, meet an important business goal, or solve a perplexing problem. Faith in our own skills and ability can keep us going long enough to meet the challenge.

Leaders need to believe in themselves for all these reasons, but they must also be able to trust the people they work with and supervise—especially when others don't. Hire the right people and let them know that you believe they can do the job. Giving them the opportunity to prove themselves builds self-confidence and strength, which can make the difference between success and failure for that individual.

With faith we can all accomplish great things in our organizations.

Leadership Tips

- Let your people know that you believe in them.

- Give your employees emotional support, especially during challenging and difficult times (personally or professionally). It is often the most important resource they need to be successful at their job.

- Learning to place your faith and trust in others is a critical part of the leadership process.

- If you truly want to become an effective leader, you must first have faith in yourself.

- If you don't have faith in yourself, don't expect others to have faith in you.

Let the people you supervise know that you have faith in them, particularly when you know that others have their doubts.

Summary

Fathers play a very important role in their children's growth and development. They protect and nurture in the crucial early years, and as their children grow and develop, they then begin the real work: helping build character and intellect. Dads also become a little tougher and more demanding as their children reach school age because they want to prepare them for the challenges that lie ahead.

The leadership lessons presented in this book remind us of the wisdom and experience fathers try to pass on to their children, so it can be applied in their adult lives. Parents are their children's first teachers *and* first leaders; what they pass on to us becomes the foundation for our own leadership development—simple lessons about life that help us prepare ourselves and our organizations for future challenges. Apply them wisely as you carry out your professional responsibilities, and remember where you learned them.

Thanks to dads everywhere for what you have taught us. We are better prepared to face the world on our own because of your leadership.

About the Author

Peter Garber, author of the ***Leadership Lessons from Life*** series of books published by HRD Press, has worked in the management and HR field for more than twenty-five years. Currently manager of equal employment opportunity for Pittsburgh-based PPG Industries, a Fortune 500 company, he has served as manager of teamwork development, director of human resources, and manager of affirmative action, using his professional experience as the basis for more than 40 books, training aids, and journal contributions. He is the author of fourteen books on management, including the current best-sellers G*iving and Receiving Performance Feedback, Turbulent Change,* and *10 Natural Forces for Business Success.*

Peter Garber's interest is in sharing what he has learned about leadership and performance management with a wide audience of organizational professionals who are searching for ways to be more effective and useful to their organizations. Prior books such as *Managing by Remote Control* and *101 Stupid Things Supervisors Do to Sabotage Success* focused on what works in well-run organizations (and what doesn't). The *Leadership Lessons from Life* books show how 21st-century professionals can tap into common life experiences to model and develop leadership qualities and skills at all levels of the organization.

Peter Garber holds an undergraduate degree in English and a master of science in personnel and guidance from the University of Pittsburgh and St. Bonaventure University, respectively. He lives with his wife Nancy and daughters Lauren and Erin in the Pittsburgh area.

He can be contacted at the following address:

Peter R. Garber
210 Edelweiss Drive
Wexford, Pennsylvania 15090
(724) 934-3173

Selected titles published by HRD Press:
Giving and Receiving Performance Feedback (2004)
Learning Points: 80 Activities and Actions for Call-Center Service Excellence (2005)
Learning Points: 100 Activities and Actions for E-Communication Excellence (2005)
Learning Points: 100 Activities and Actions for Customer Service Excellence (2005)
15 Reproducible Activities for Reinforcing Business Ethics and Values (2005)
25 Reproducible Activities for Customer Service Excellence (2005)